OVER 10 WAYS TO MAKE MONEY AND GET OUT OF DEBT

BY

ZETH KRAUSE

www.youtube.com/user/zethystar

If you are wanting to have money you first need to start thinking like your a poor person. You know how they say the more money you make the more you spend? Well it is true. Here is some verses from the Bible about money.

(Proverbs 17:16 Of what use is money in the hand of a fool, since he has no desire to get wisdom?)
 (Luke 14:28 Suppose one of you wants to build a tower. Will he not first sit down and estimate the cost to see if he has enough money to complete it?)
(Proverbs 10:4 Lazy hands make a man poor, but diligent hands bring wealth.)

Before you get into debt build extra income or if your already in debt I'll show you ways to get out of it.

1. NOT IN DEBT

If you aren't in debt yet and still live with your parents. I wouldn't go out and buy a house, rent or an expensive car but save your money and make an extra income. I am going to show you easy ways in this guide book and a lot of them you don't even need money to do. If you need to buy a place to live in soon read. #2 IN DEBT

2. IN DEBT

If you are in debt you need to start out with selling as much stuff that you don't need. (Ebay, Craigeslist, Yardsale, Newspaper, Facebook). Just to name a few ways to sell your stuff. You need to start thinking about what you can live without or what do you really use. If you have a house payment that is dragging you down you need to sell it. If you really want to get out of your situation you might need to go extreme to build your wealth and get out of debt but these things weren't extreme less then a 100 years ago. A lot of people might think you are crazy but you will be free and they will still be living pay check to pay check. You need to ask yourself why you are wanting to get out of debt and Set some goals. It could be that you want to work for yourself and be free to do what you want when you want or you just want extra money to help people out. If I tell you how to do this and you don't do what I am telling you to do it is not because it don't work its because you don't want it bad enough. OK! You ask how do I do this. Well I have a few ways. You can live in a camper, trailer, or a small cabin until you build extra wealth or build your own business instead of throwing all your money away on a house payment or rent.

WHAT CAN I DO TO MAKE MONEY?

www.youtube.com/user/zethystar

1.Have you ever wanted to write a book and get it published? Well I will show you how to do it for free. First you need to write a book and it can be about anything. Examples (children, cooking, learning, guide) just about anything you can think of. If you need illustrations you can have them made for you. One site that will do this is (**www.Fiverr.com**). Make sure the book is not copied from anyone else's work cause they won't publish it because it goes against copy right laws. I would start with an easy children's book they are really easy to make. After you have got everything done with your book and ready to publish it for free go to (www.Createspace.com **and kdp.amazon.com**) You can make really good money doing this.

2. Want to get your music or movie published for free and make money off of it? Well first make sure it is all your own work so you don't get in-trouble for copy right. You can publish on (**itunes and createspace.com**).

3.Have you ever wanted to make a game or an App and publish it for free on every cell phone and game console? Same goes with this make sure its your own work so you don't get in-trouble for copy right. Ok here we go (For android **www.developer.android.com**) (For apple **developer.apple.com**) (For playstation **www.playstation.com/en-us/develop/**) (For xbox **www.xbox.com/en-US/developers**) (For nintendo **https://wiiu-developers.nintendo.com/**). Go start making money.

4.If you don't know how to make an app or game you can have one made for you and you will make all the money. This is my favorite (**http://www.chupamobile.com/**) but you can just search app source code to find more.

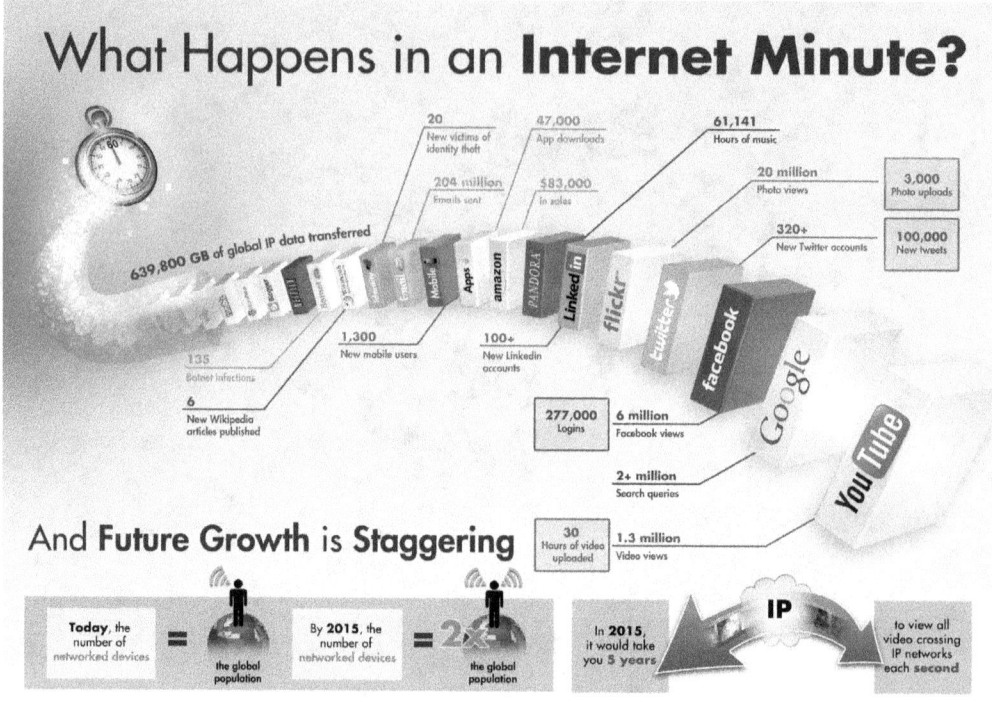

What Happens in an **Internet Minute?**

639,800 GB of global IP data transferred

20
New victims of identity theft

204 million
Emails sent

47,000
App downloads

583,000
in sales

61,141
Hours of music

20 million
Photo views

3,000
Photo uploads

320+
New Twitter accounts

100,000
New tweets

1,300
New mobile users

100+
New Linkedin accounts

135
Botnet infections

6
New Wikipedia articles published

277,000
Logins

6 million
Facebook views

2+ million
Search queries

And **Future Growth** is **Staggering**

30
Hours of video uploaded

1.3 million
Video views

Today, the number of networked devices = the global population

By **2015**, the number of networked devices = 2× the global population

In **2015**, it would take you 5 years

IP

to view all video crossing IP networks each second

---

5. Make money making YouTube videos. You need a Google adsense and a Google adword account after you do that you will have to monetize your YouTube account.

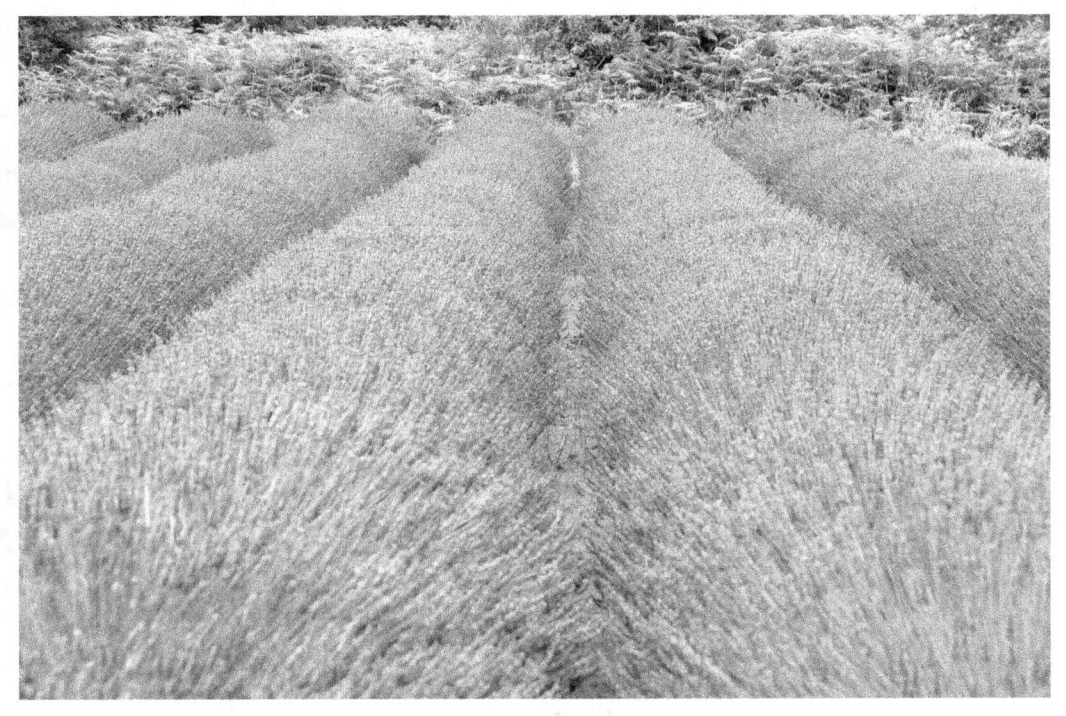

6.Grow something to sell. Lots of people are making a lot of money off of
small and cheap garden farms. Some of the things they grow are Bamboo, Lavender, Trees, mushrooms, hemp and tons of other things. You can make stuff with some of these things to sell or just sell as it is.

7. Make money by selling or renting homes. Have you ever seen those shipping containers they have on those cargo ships? Well you can make a good and very cheap home out of them and sell or rent it out. You can also build one with sand bags they call them earth bag homes. A shipping container home that is 1,500sqft can be built for around 10,000 to 20,000 dollars and a 2,000sqft earth bag for around 5,000 to 10,000 this isn't including all the extras you may include this is just basic stuff but you would make a great profit off of them.

8. Buy stuff in bulk and sell it on ebay.com or amazon.com. Like (www.AliExpress.com) (www.Alibaba.com) (www.Chinabuye.com) (www.ebay.com).

When you buy stuff in bulk make sure you test the product out before you go crazy and spend a ton of money on the product. Most of the stuff I have bought have been really good product but I have had a few that weren't. Make sure you come up with a good item that people want to buy.

SOCIAL MEDIA

10. Help advertise for others and get paid for everything you sell. You won't have to pay for anything to do this. Go and make an account with (www.Clickbank.com) this is just one of them I trust.

11. If you like taking photos and would like to make money with them well you can download an app called (Foap) or websites (www.Fineartamerica.com) (www.istockphoto.com) (www.Shutterfly.com)

12. Put up solar panels, wind turbines or water generators and hook it up and sell the extra power to the power company. Call your local power company to see what you have to do first. A lot of the local power companies are contract companies that are run by a big power company.

Donate

13. If you would like to make money playing video games for a living start a twitch account and live stream your game play or you talking about a game but don't forget to put a Paypal donation button on your twitch account.

14. Right now people are looking for a cheap place to live so if you got in to the tiny home trend and started building them I think you would make a really good living off of building them.

15. If you live in a state that has medical marijuana. Get the growing card and you can sell it. For more info about this go to my youtube channel. Www.youtube.com/zethystar

16. Make your own drink company for around 10,000 to 30,000. I know that sounds like a lot but it isn't for your own drink company. One of the web sites to get your equipment is www.alibaba.com

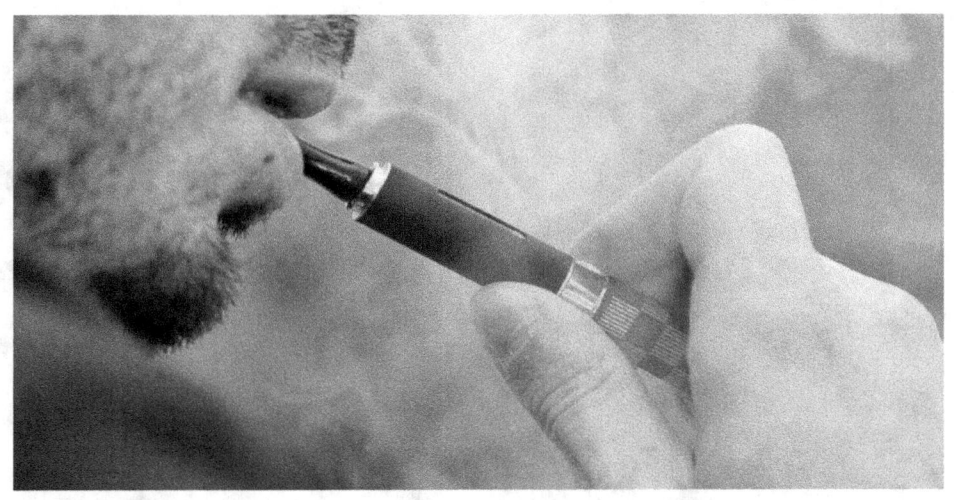

17. Start an E cig business it is easy and pretty cheap to get started. You could sell them to gas stations, facebook, newspaper or open your own store. I would do my own search for e cigs on google because there is a lot of companies out there but I am going start checking out some of these companies and letting you guys know what ones I like. Www.youtube.com/zethystar

18. Sell insurance for Motor Club of America and get plenty of benefits for doing it you can get more info   here (www.mymcapro.com/buildfreedom)

How to stay out of debt

www.youtube.com/user/zethystar

First off you want to make your money make money for you and not to spend more money then you have. I would make a second income and stay at the job you have now and use that second income to build it up so you can quite your job and come home and start running your new business full time. If you have to put money into your business don't put all of you money in to it take baby steps. When you start making money reinvest it and keep building it up also get rid of debt you don't need and use that extra money to grow your business. Once you get out of debt you will never want to put yourself in to debt again and when you get completely out of debt you will have even more money and free to do what you want. Most already know all these things I am saying but sometimes you just need to be reminded.

www.youtube.com/user/zethystar